A MAN'S IMAGE AND IDENTITY

*A Study in a Man's
Pathway to Christ-likeness
in Today's Society*

by JACK HAYFORD

Published by Living Way Ministries
14300 Sherman Way
Van Nuys, CA (USA) 91405-2499
(818) 779-8180 • (800) 776-8180

ISBN 0-916847-13-6
Printed in the United States of America

This message was originally brought at The Church On The Way.

It has since been edited and revised for publication by Pastor Hayford, in partnership with Pastor Bob Anderson, Director of Pastoral Relations.

The audio cassette of this message (#00295) may be purchased from:

Living Way Ministries
14300 Sherman Way
Van Nuys, CA 91405

TABLE OF CONTENTS

Chapter One
THE POWER OF IMAGES

Images.

They're everywhere.

While living on this high-concept, visually-oriented techno-planet, we're virtually suffocated by images of all kinds.

- From advertising;
- from TV;
- from movies;
- from billboards and newspapers and magazines . . . a deluge of images pours daily into our lives.

And they stick with us. From the image factory of entertainment and news, images of faces and events scorch the memory for years and years. That's verified by the fact that it takes no effort for any of us to recall the exact images of:

- The explosion of the space shuttle Challenger at take-off;
- John F. Kennedy clutching his throat while riding in a Dallas motorcade;
- Neil Armstrong's first step onto the lunar surface;
- The eerie luminescent missile contrails raining on Baghdad during the first eve of Desert Storm.

Images have the power to live on in our minds for a lifetime.

But that's not all.

Images also have the power to shape us.

Complete image systems like those architected by advertising agencies and styled by society's values forge their own icons that affect us by their persistent tutorial nature. They continually spew forth informally announced but very real social standards by which we tend to measure our lives--standards which determine how well we are conforming to everyone else; standards which determine things from what is "politically correct," to what is "acceptable behavior" in this "brave new world order." If image competition doesn't compel us to have a car nicer than the neighbors, then it will motivate us to subtly inform a lunch gathering about the social "note-worthy" we had to dinner last night. Or it may incite us to go out of our way to let people know just how well our kids are doing at their Ivy League school. Or maybe it's falling to the temptation to spend more than we should on the latest fashions with money that should have gone into ministry.

Teenagers, for example, have suffered with some of the most severe and blatant degenerations of peer-image-pressure ever. The simple label of the clothing they wear to school is often a critical factor which establishes their worth as human beings among their peers. Worse, in recent years, the image of being "cool" is now sometimes secured in urban high school social circles by having a condom tucked away in the wallet--ready for action. Even if it was never used, the "illusion of coolness" is still sought--and obtained--by nothing more than the possession of so unworthy a symbol.

At every age of life, the pressurized process that comes from a world filled with images is basically the same. It's a cyclical process. We're not only drawn to *ingest* those images from the world around us, we're also being programmed to *project* those same images in our living in order to be accepted as "one of the crowd." The world spirit of comparison and competition is fierce, virtually compelling us to wear the label, look the look, talk the talk, join the pack--and so often, to compromise our morals. In short, "look" just like the world-image dictates.

The real stinger is, *image* is not just a *look*.

It's a design of *thought*.

It's a pattern of *values*.

Image is not just surface layering--what we look like--it's substantive stuff. It touches the core of our being.

For example: If a person said they opposed abortion in *any* way, in most secular circles scorn and ridicule can be guaranteed. The reason: you aren't conforming to the "correct" way of thought; you aren't taking on their *image*. The point is that hosts of issues today are ground into the fabric of our minds--whether we like it or not. And it's crucial to identify, because the issue of *image* in our lives extends to that which governs the *way we live* and *what we think* and *who we are.*

Illustration:

Picture a digital watch. Instead of mainsprings and gears, it runs on a very tiny circuit of computer-technology origin. That circuit was literally a photograph--*an image*--before it ever kept time. First, the pathways of logic were drawn with ink on paper; the circuit was designed as an image. This image determined how the electrical current would flow and what it would do throughout all the intersections, avenues, roads, and courses that would eventually form the electronic circuit. This *image* was designed to *DO something*; in this case, it was designed to keep time.

Next, the design of this circuit image was photographed on high resolution film and reduced to a micro-sized version. Taking the multiple components of that tiny film image, it was then layered into a *physical* composite imprint, i.e., a computer chip. This imprinted "circuit" then became the works of the watch. So what started out as a mere *photographic image* ended up being a *functional machine.*

Similarly, if I choose to take, for example, a pro-life stand on the moral issue of abortion, it's because my view of God's image in each human has imprinted a circuit of behavior which, to use our illustration, has made me a "functional machine" in the interest of the unborn. The reverse is true, as is the application to anything shaping the thinking of people in our society. Each mind is a kind of working logic system similar to a computer chip: it generates a pattern of behavior, a circuit of response, a network of conclusions--all according to the *image* burned into the circuitry. (And most of us learn early, if we don't conform to the world's *image* on a subject, we are certain to meet with disapproval.) Therefore:

• *Image* is more than surface, pretense, showy stuff.

• *Image* generates decisions every hour.

• *Image* can determine a person's future.

As the Bible says, "As a person thinks in his heart, so is he." A paraphrase might read, "According to the circuit image in a person's heart, that's how he or she will make decisions in life."

Image is potent stuff. And it's quite an expansive topic, but with very critical and specific applications to a man's life in Christ.

So how do we, as men of God, approach the topic of *image* as it pertains to our lives in Christ, and how do we conform to the right image in the most effective way while resisting the world's image? The initial step requires us to analyze the chief forces that stand at the ready to either conform us into God's image or to hinder that process. Understanding those forces and the full impact of the word "image" is the beginning point of our study.

In approaching the topic of A MAN'S IMAGE, we're pressing deeper than simply denouncing materialism and immorality while puffing-up high-toned religiosity. We're saying *more* than, "Let the *world* take their yachts and latest Rodeo Drive fashions, Mercedes logo on the hood, arrogant walk and air of sophistication, immoral conquests, and filthy films." And we're saying more than contrived religious images--pretentious fastings, displayed generosity in offerings done before the eyes of man. Instead, our focus is simple and direct: it's on Jesus! And Jesus has everything to do with *image*.

When Genesis 1:26 announces that "God created man in His own *image*," *image* suddenly becomes a very spiritual topic which deserves to be understood and must be reckoned with. The Bible makes it clear: *Image* is more than making a good impression; more than having certain clothes or a new hairstyle; more than a shallow facade of acceptability, as if social acceptance were the equivalent of substance and character.

Image conveys:
- likeness and resemblance
- functional behavior
- decision-making dynamics

Therefore, image is:
* *identity*
* *character*
* *destiny*.

Unfortunately, as we'll see, God's original blueprint for us as men--His Chief Designer *image*--has been distorted, mangled, and continues to be transmitted in a damaged condition. We'll discuss several diverse forces that impose failure upon God's intended image for humanity, but the initial and instigating one is common to every human being: Sin. The Fall. The ruined circuitry.

In even greater power than sneezes or shoe sizes, Adam's DNA--with his fallen image--envelopes us. Cast millenniums ago when Adam chose not to heed God's voice, but instead confirmed allegiance to the lying serpent, the devil, his fallen image is still as fresh today as it was back then in the Garden--reproduced now with every newborn baby emerging from the womb. Bequeathed to us through inheritance, this is an image of sin, brokenness, and failure that produces our:

* irresponsibility to obey God's holy laws;
* incapacity to fulfill our God-ordained destinies;
* inability to enjoy life as God intended it to be.

Consequently, we live in a society, a race, that needs massive amounts of repair.

There are broken images of lives every-where. How things appear in the human race, the image of how life is in this present world, is not how God originally designed it to be. Life as it is now isn't according to the original circuit image designed for man in Heaven.

There's been a short-circuit of that design.

Augmenting this negative influence of Adam's fallen nature in us are several other forces which have an image system all their own. They are seeking to establish their circuitry as the image-making device in our personality. Some of those forces come at us from the mere nature of the human condition; other forces come from a con-trived, strategic, intentional effort of hell to ruin lives--sometimes by subtle means, other times by the bold and brash. Put all these dynamics together in the same life-time of experience and you've got a struggle on your hands.

The good news is, we aren't locked into a fatalistic pre-determined destiny. The bad news is: we have two destinies await-ing us, both of which are in conflict with one another, both vying for our allegiance by reaching to us with their *images*; (1) the natural out-working of all our inheritance in *Adam's fallen image*; and (2) the destiny dynamically unfolding to us through the *image of Christ*--a potential for us all when we received Him as our Lord and Savior.

Christ's Person, powerfully growing within us, can restore the image of God in our manliness, and a circuitry which is diametrically opposed to the fallen image of Adam can be ours.

Exposure to the Imprint

But in order for the image of Christ to be successfully imprinted upon us and within us, *we* must participate in the process. *We* have to do something. We have to *commit* to an ongoing, sufficient *EXPOSURE to the living God.* Let me explain by means of a simple but beautiful analogy.

The first known photograph was made in 1816 by Joseph Niepce. But long before that, it's almost as though we're listening to a description of the photographic process in the Old Testament, three thousand years before Niepce produced his first image!

> *They looked to Him and were radiant, and their faces were not ashamed.* Psalm 34:5

A friend pointed out the photographic process in this verse to me. Let me share it.

• *"They"* (the film--that which would receive an image)

• *"looked"* (exposure)

• *"to Him"* (the source of Light)

• *"and were radiant"* (bore a resemblance to that to which they had been exposed).

And the resulting photographic exhibition was successful: *"their faces were not ashamed."*

Here is another 3,000-year-old "Kodak moment" from King David:

> *As for me, I will see Your face*
> *in righteousness; I shall be*
> *satisfied when I   awake in*
> *Your likeness.   Psalm 17:15*

It's divine photography. *Image* produced by Light. (Some things never change!) And God's Spirit is yearning to engage us in a whole new reshaping process: to transform us from the broken image incurred by the Fall and propel us toward the liberating, glorious image of Christ, the Founder of the Original Image. But this process requires that we let God's light--the truth of His Word--shine into our souls. It's *that* exposure:

- an open heart
- a receptive attitude
- a mind alive to *Him*
- a humbled soul

There's where the new image can be imprinted.

Chapter Two
MEN RESISTING
THE WORLD IMAGE

It's one of the Top 10 Stories of all time!

All the elements are present. The episode of The Fiery Furnace, taken from the pages of God's Word, not only commands our attention by its raw excitement, but it's loaded with insight into how the "world" seeks to impose its image on *any* man in *any* generation. Although the story takes place in Babylon--the ancient world's image of cultural and commercial success--and though it's distanced from us by nearly twenty-five centuries in time, it's as contemporary as today's newscast.

To get it all, it's best to read the first three chapters of the prophetic book of Daniel. But for inclusion here I'm only presenting that portion of the text which provides the essential support for the key points we're studying.

OVERVIEW: The time was 606 B.C. World power was in the grip of Nebuchadnezzar, Emperor of Babylon. This City was the essence of cultural advancement, military power, economic dominance, and spiritual idolatry. Located near today's Iraqi Capital of Baghdad, it commanded a realm reaching from today's Persian Gulf to the Mediterranean Sea.

When the Babylonian troops lay siege to

Jerusalem, Capital of Judea, the Judean Kingdom collapses. As part of the spoils of war, Nebuchadnezzar takes some of the nation's finest, most intelligent young men back to Babylon, to train them for service in the King's Court. The best known are Daniel, Shadrach, Meshach, and Abednego.

There are three steps in unfolding the story: The Capture and Training; The King's Dream and Interpretation; The King's Image and Confrontation. These three steps issue in the fiery furnace event and the miraculous deliverance of the committed young men. Here is the abbreviated presentation:

I. The Capture and Training (Daniel 1:1-21)

II. The King's Dream and Interpretation (Daniel 2:1-49)

III. The King's Image and Confrontation (Daniel 3:1-18)

Conclusion: The Fiery Furnace and Miracle Deliverance (Daniel 3:19-30)

The Abbreviated Text: Daniel 1-3

CHAPTER 1: In the third year of the reign of Jehoiakim king of Judah, Nebuchadnezzar king of Babylon came to Jerusalem and besieged it. And the Lord gave Jehoiakim king of Judah into his hand . . . Then the king instructed Ashpenaz, the master of his eunuchs, to bring some of the . . . young men in whom there was no

18

blemish, but good-looking, gifted in all wisdom, possessing knowledge and quick to understand, who had ability to serve in the king's palace, and whom they might teach the language and literature of the Chaldeans. And the king appointed for them a daily provision of the king's delicacies and of the wine which he drank, and three years of training for them, so that at the end of that time they might serve before the king.

Now from among those of the sons of Judah were Daniel, Hananiah, Mishael, and Azariah. To them the chief of the eunuchs gave names: he gave Daniel the name Belteshazzar; to Hananiah, Shadrach; to Mishael, Meshach; and to Azariah, Abed-Nego. But Daniel purposed in his heart that he would not defile himself with the portion of the king's delicacies, nor with the wine which he drank; therefore he requested of the chief of the eunuchs that he might not defile himself . . .

And the chief of the eunuchs said to Daniel, "I fear my lord the king, who has appointed your food and drink. For why should he see your faces looking worse than the young men who are your age? Then you would endanger my head before the king."

So Daniel said . . . "Please test your servants for ten days, and let them give us vegetables to eat and water to drink. Then let our appearance be examined before you . . ."

So he consented with them in this matter, and tested them ten days. And at the end of ten days their features appeared better . . .

As for these four young men, God gave them knowledge and skill in all literature and wisdom; and Daniel had understanding in all visions and dreams.

Now at the end of the days, when the king had said that they should be brought in . . . the king interviewed them, and among them all none was found like Daniel, Hananiah, Mishael, and Azariah; therefore they served before the king.

CHAPTER 2: Now in the second year of Nebuchadnezzar's reign, Nebuchadnezzar had dreams; and his spirit was so troubled that his sleep left him. Then the king gave the command to call the magicians, the astrologers, the sorcerers, and the Chaldeans to tell the king his dreams. So they came and stood before the king. And the king said to them, "I have had a dream, and my spirit is anxious to know the dream." Then the Chaldeans spoke to the king in Aramaic, "O king, live forever! Tell your servants the dream, and we will give the interpretation." The king answered and said to the Chaldeans, "My decision is firm: if you do not make known the dream to me, and its interpretation, you shall be cut in pieces, and your houses shall be made an ash heap."

The Chaldeans answered the king, and said, "There is not a man on earth who can tell the king's matter; therefore no king, lord, or ruler has ever asked such things of any magician, astrologer, or Chaldean . . . and there is no other who can tell it to the king except the gods, whose dwelling is not with flesh." For this reason the king . . . gave a command to destroy all the wise men of Babylon.

Then with counsel and wisdom Daniel answered Arioch, the captain of the king's guard . . . he answered and said to Arioch the king's captain, "Why is the decree from the king so urgent?"

Then Arioch made the decision known to Daniel. So Daniel went in and asked the king to give him time, that he might tell the king the interpretation. Then Daniel went to his house, and made the decision known to Hananiah, Mishael, and Azariah, his companions, that they might seek mercies from the God of heaven concerning this secret, so that Daniel and his companions might not perish with the rest of the wise men of Babylon. Then the secret was revealed to Daniel in a night vision. So Daniel blessed the God of heaven.

Then Arioch quickly brought Daniel before the king, and said thus to him, "I have found a man of the captives of Judah, who will make known to the king the interpretation."

Daniel answered in the presence of the king: ". . . there is a God in heaven who reveals secrets, and He has made known to King Nebuchadnezzar what will be in the latter days . . .

"You, O king, were watching; and behold, a great image! This great image, whose splendor was excellent, stood before you; and its form was awesome. This image's head was of fine gold, its chest and arms of silver, its belly and thighs of bronze, its legs of iron, its feet partly of iron and partly of clay. You watched while a stone was cut out without hands, which struck the image on its feet of iron and clay, and broke them in pieces.

"This is the dream. Now we will tell the interpretation of it before the king. You, O king, are a king of kings. For the God of heaven has given you a kingdom, power, strength, and glory . . . you are this head of gold. But after you shall arise another kingdom inferior to yours; then another, a third kingdom of bronze, which shall rule over all the earth. And the fourth kingdom shall be as strong as iron, inasmuch as iron breaks in pieces and shatters everything; and like iron that crushes, that kingdom will break in pieces and crush all the others.

"And as the toes of the feet were partly of iron and partly of clay, so the kingdom shall be partly strong and partly fragile. As you saw iron mixed with ceramic clay, they will mingle with the seed of men; but they will not adhere to one another, just as iron does not mix with clay. And in the days of these kings the God of heaven will set up a kingdom which shall never be destroyed... and it shall stand forever . . . the great God has made known to the king what will come to pass after this. The dream is certain, and its interpretation is sure."

Then King Nebuchadnezzar fell on his face, prostrate before Daniel . . . and said, "Truly your God is the God of gods, the Lord of kings, and a revealer of secrets, since you could reveal this secret." Then the king promoted Daniel and gave him many great gifts; and he made him ruler over the whole province of Babylon, and chief administrator over all the wise men of Babylon. Also Daniel petitioned the king, and he set Shadrach, Meshach, and Abed-Nego over the affairs of the province of Babylon; but Daniel sat in the gate of the king.

CHAPTER 3: Nebuchadnezzar the king made an image of gold, whose height was sixty cubits and its width six cubits. He set it up in the plain of Dura, in the province of Babylon. And King Nebuchadnezzar sent word to gather together . . . all the officials of the provinces gathered together for the dedication of the image . . .

Then a herald cried aloud: "To you it is commanded, O peoples, nations, and languages, that at the time you hear the sound of the music, you shall fall down and worship the gold image that King Nebuchadnezzar has set up; and whoever does not fall down and worship shall be cast immediately into the midst of a burning fiery furnace."

Therefore at that time certain Chaldeans

came forward and accused the Jews. They spoke and said to King Nebuchadnezzar, "There are certain Jews whom you have set over the affairs of the province of Babylon: Shadrach, Meshach, and Abed-Nego; these men, O king, have not paid due regard to you. They do not serve your gods or worship the gold image which you have set up." [Daniel was apparently away on a court mission at this time.]

Then Nebuchadnezzar, in rage and fury, gave the command to bring Shadrach, Meshach, and Abed-Nego. So they brought these men before the king. Nebuchadnezzar spoke, saying to them, "Is it true that you do not . . . worship the gold image which I have set up? If you do not worship, you shall be cast immediately into the midst of a burning fiery furnace. And who is the god who will deliver you from my hands?" Shadrach, Meshach, and Abed-Nego answered, "O Nebuchadnezzar, we have no need to answer you in this matter. If that is the case, our God whom we serve is able to deliver us from the burning fiery furnace, and He will deliver us from your hand, O king. But if not, let it be known to you, O king, that we do not serve your gods, nor will we worship the gold image which you have set up."

Then Nebuchadnezzar was full of fury, and the expression on his face changed toward (them) . . .

And he commanded certain men of his army to bind and cast them into the burning *fiery furnace. Then these men were bound in their garments, and were cast into the midst of the burning fiery furnace.*

Then King Nebuchadnezzar was astonished; and he rose in haste and spoke, saying to his counselors, "Did we not cast three men bound into the midst of the fire?" They answered and said to the king, "True, O king." "Look!" he answered, "I see four men loose, walking in the midst of the fire; and they are not hurt, and the form of the fourth is like the Son of God." Then Nebuchadnezzar went near the mouth of the burning fiery furnace and spoke, saying, "Shadrach, Meshach, and Abed-Nego, servants of the Most High God, come out, and come here." Then (they) came from the midst of the fire. And the satraps, administrators, governors, and the king's counselors gathered together, and they saw these men on whose bodies the fire had no power; the hair of their head was not singed nor were their garments affected, and the smell of fire was not on them. Nebuchadnezzar spoke, saying, "Blessed be the God of Shadrach, Meshach, and Abed-Nego, who sent His Angel and delivered His servants who trusted in Him, and they have frustrated the king's word, and yielded their bodies, that they should not serve nor worship any god except their own God! . . . There is no other God who can deliver like this." Then the king promoted Shadrach, Meshach, and Abed-Nego in the province of Babylon.

In every way this is a story *of* men *for* men to *shape* men!

• It begins with four men caught in the vice of circumstance, being called to conformity to a human system governed by the then-most-powerful man in the world, King Nebuchadnezzar.

• It continues with men demonstrating a faith which determines to become *effective* within the system, but *not* to be *shaped* by it.

• The story turns a corner and we see a man dream of God's purpose for His life; a dream he at first doesn't understand.

• Answering his dilemma is another man; one who knows God and is able to speak into the life of a man (even his king) with the truth of God's purpose.

• At this point we discover a man (the king) who supposes that he is the one who can bring God's purpose about in his life by his own wisdom and power. His pride cultivates a self-image which he seeks to use to intimidate others.

• While the majority in the system bow to the image-intimidation, a distinct band of men refuses, knowing the call to *bow* to the system is different from *serving* in the system. Their faith and spiritual commitment is put to the test. They honor God first!

• When these men "face the heat," the

result is God's divine intervention, and the confounding of all onlookers as God steps into their situation and vindicates them.

*   *   *   *   *

I don't know that there is any incident in God's Word that more specifically or clearly addresses the pressures which a believing man will face today. The world system is structured by the same satanic spirit which motivated Nebuchadnezzar. That's the reason the Book of Revelation uses the name of ancient Babylon to symbolize and summarize the whole of all global commerce and corruption that will eventually come to its demise. Look at the parallels in the story which reveal the kind of "image-pressures" which a man faces today.

1. "Your only worth is to serve the system."
When the four young men are taken to Babylon for training, there is no regard for anything else than what they can bring to the king's program. There is no regard for any value other than the "meat on the hoof" value of each man's ability to serve the interests of the business.

IMPACT: *The world system will seek to reduce your view of your worth to your ability to succeed on its terms.*

2. "Your identity is not yours to determine."

The renaming of the four young men is powerfully significant. The abolishing of their born identity reflects the will of the system to not only *re*-locate (geographically) but to *dis*-locate (psychologically). Study also will disclose the fact that each of the four names contained a form of the Name of the God of Israel: Dani*EL*, Hanani*YAH*, Azari*YAH*, and Misha*EL*. Further, the names they were given were each related to Babylonian deities--demon gods worshiped in that culture. It's a classic ploy of our Adversary to seek to put his stamp on your life, your mind, your work.

IMPACT: *The world will seek to link your identity with its operations and remove your association with anything remotely related to God, His way, or His will.*

3. "Feed and feast on our delicacies."

Imagine, if you will, the heaping "training table" which was set before the team of young men which had been gathered from the several nations Nebuchadnezzar had conquered. They were not only survivors from their separate cultures, but they were given preferred treatment and the opportunity to "make it big in the big city." The table set before them--a menu which contained food prohibited in the Jewish culture from which Daniel and his partners had come--becomes a testing point. Will they let their tastes be determined by the society around them, or will they keep their self-control intact and trust God to make them successful anyway?

IMPACT: *Whether it's the call to employ the devious methods used in the corporation, the three-cocktail lunch, or the feast at the office party, today's man faces the decision as to what forces will shape him: the "spread" on the outside, or the "Spirit" on the inside.*

4. "Is there anybody here who really has touch with God?"

The second chapter of Daniel is a dual study in God's dealings with men. On the one hand, His unfolding of His sovereign purpose to Nebuchadnezzar tells us:

A. God speaks to any and every man, even though the man may himself not have a true knowledge of Him. God's imprint seeks to register truth on every human soul, and each man must determine what response he will show to the Creator's revelation to his mind and being (see Romans 1:18-2:11).

B. God uses the man who is faithful to Him to penetrate the confusion of the world's inability to understand His purpose, and to make him an interpreter of His ways, His truth, and His power.

IMPACT: *When a man resists the world system's shaping him, but still serves within*

29

that system with wisdom, he is destined to become a shaper of thinking in that realm which couldn't shape him. The world is seeking men who really have touch with God!

5. "Face the music and dance or you'll face the heat and die!"

When the king builds the image and calls everyone to worship at his command, we have the clearest picture possible of the world system's seeking to pour a man in its mold. And it's all being spearheaded by a man who depicts the world system's way of a man demonstrating his authority. Nebuchadnezzar is the picture of the typical man who (a) has an inner sense of destiny but who only thinks it can be fulfilled by *mastering* other people, rather than *serving* them. And he equally depicts any of us men who (b) become infuriated whenever our will or whim isn't bowed to by those we seek to dominate. There are considerable issues for us to confront in ourselves if we find either of these world-traits in our lives as believers.

But foremost at this point of the biblical narrative is the incredible faith of the three young men. (Daniel's absence doesn't suggest he surrendered to the system. You can read of his own personal response to a similar situation in Daniel 6.) Here, this trio "faces the music," but refuses to bow to its call. Their response brings intense fire upon their heads, but amid their fiery circumstance the Lord Himself comes to walk with them and to deliver them.

IMPACT: *The truth within you, incarnated in your commitment to its moral and spiritual demands, will outlast any flame of human fury or fashioning.*

What "Worldliness" Is

The real evil of worldliness is that the world spirit is committed to trying to stamp its image upon and within us. Worldliness means world*like*ness. It means adopting the world's value system.

And we're all vulnerable.

The temptation to succumb to the world's image is often severe. Sometimes the circumstance of your associations or employment *demands* that you conform to its image or your very survival in the system will be threatened. That's what happened to these three men who stood before the king in ancient Babylon, but they "faced the music," survived the flames, and wouldn't buy into the world image. They refused conformity to the "circuit" of values and behavior the system sought to "imprint"--to *image* them with.

When the Scripture reports they were commanded to "worship" the golden image, it does not mean they were to just fall down before a golden spike and salute. Rather they were to yield to the image's system, *swear allegiance* to it, to accept a "circuit" engraved inside them--to worship a spiritual icon of an alien kingdom.

Don't miss the picture! Nebuchadnezzar is a type of Satan--the arch-manipulator of the world system. He's the one that sits at hell's Master Controls and from that location exerts massive pressure throughout the globe to conform mankind--one at a time--into his own image. The plan is well-coordinated and administrated efficiently, as hosts of spiritual powers move invisibly among mankind to enlist "buyers" into the system.

People who are without God have the universal human proclivity to worship, a desire to "know" *something* or *someone* in one form or another which gives life meaning and fulfillment. However, more often than not, the worldling ends up in a worship of self-will and self-protective interest, following anyone who makes pride and self attainment an object of homage as an image to be served.

Satan, of course, is the arch-proponent of pride and self-will's self-serving way. His style is to so smoothly arrange the "music"--the call to *his* system's values--that each person thinks he has chosen this course on his own: "I did it *my* way."

There are custom-made approaches, too. If a man isn't assailed by the pressure to participate in a world-system of worship born out of *pride* (self-righteousness, in-

flated ego, or a sense of macho superiority),
then the Master Manipulator has other tac-
tics. He'll lure the soul to worship a system
that gives rewards, pleasure, or "freedom
from threat" if you just bow down to the
system's image. In one form or another, the
world's system of "worship"--requiring obei-
sance to its image--is either seductive, coer-
cive, or blinding. It *never* has in mind the
ultimate blessing of its devotees. Its intent
is solely on their destruction, for Satan, as
the prince of this world, hates the prospect
of any man bearing God's image, and with
vitriolic wrath seeks to control people and
remove any hope for that true image's recov-
ery.

There's a marvelous added lesson which
we must not miss amid the triumph of faith
this episode reveals. Read again the response of the three to the king's threat of the
furnace:

> *If that is the case, our God
> whom we serve is able to de-
> liver us from the burning fiery
> furnace, and He will deliver us
> from your hand, O king.*
>
> *BUT IF NOT, let it be known to
> you, O king, that we do not
> serve your gods, nor will we
> worship the gold image which
> you have set up.*
> Daniel 3:17-18
> (emphasis added)

I love the way they phrased that challenge. "Our God is going to deliver us from the fiery furnace. BUT IF HE DOESN'T ... we're *not* going to serve you anyway!"

There's a beauty in the humility manifested by these men.

Listen, these are great men of faith! But they don't pretend omniscience. They acknowledge they're just like you and me-- human and vulnerable. They feel no need for bravado: "Hey, Neb! You pagan dingo!! Let us show you what REAL power is!!"

No sir! They admit they have no guarantee on the outcome of their boss's decision, but they're going to serve the Lord. Can you see how this liberates you and me to say, "The Lord's going to see me through, *but if He doesn't do it the way I might expect* Him to, or the way I hope He will, or on my timetable--I'm *still* going to trust Him anyway!" It reminds me of Job's words, "Even if God Himself slays me, I'll still trust Him!"

There is a place of trust where any man can rest in the Lord . . . *no matter what!*

• Knowing God's beyond-genius and omniscient wisdom is supporting you;

• Convinced of His beyond-computer design of His redemptive purpose in you; and

• Comforted by His beyond-imagination eternal love for you, commit yourself to such eternal faithfulness and let male ego and self-reliance take a back seat.

A Set-Up

I can't escape this recurrent phrase, "he set it up": "the king had set up" (3:2); "Nebuchadnezzar had set up" (v.3); "the king had set up" (v. 5); "the king had set up" (v. 7).

Listen to it. *The image situation was a "set-up"!* It's the colloquial term we use for scams, conspiracies, and traps. So it is we'll find the adversary's plan is always "set up" to put you down, trip you up, or topple you over; set up to force your compromise. We face a world of set-ups which are set up:

• to come down at times with intimidating force;

• to seek to etch a different image on our souls;

• to define our identity on the system's terms;

• to compel conformity to behavior alien to our highest call in life.

But three men--living in an era exactly like yours and mine--did more than survive. They impacted and imaged the society which was trying to stamp its image on them! A furnace, heated up to a blinding blaze and intended to reduce them to ashes, was mastered by the might of the Master who walked with them through the flames. Please note this, brother: It's *in* the fire you'll often find the nearest and dearest fellowship with Jesus!! And note also, when it was all over, Nebuchadnezzar could only admit: "There's no god like the God of these men!"

Chapter Three
DECODING THE ENCODED EFFORT AT RECODING THE FIRST CODE

The title's a mouthful, I admit. But it touches the nerve of an idea that needs to be central to the understanding of every man, and that sentence--serving as title to this chapter--says it all. You and I are living out our lives in a setting where two powers wrestle to control us: God, to *restore* us; Satan, to *destroy* us. The key for each of the two is to communicate to us--to get the message through that says, "Everything's better if you do it my way." The problem in our communication with God is that our human receiving unit has been jumbled, and doesn't receive as clearly from the Manufacturer (God) as it does from the Manipulator (Satan).

Let me "decode" the title.

First, by proper definition, a code is "a systematically arranged, comprehensive set of laws"; and also, "a set of signals used to transmit messages." In a word, there is an imprinted "image" of the world's "laws and signals" which has been burned into the mind of each soul which has ever lived in sin--and we all have. This was not the original circuitry (which now has been damaged)--the original "image" of clarity in understanding God's "laws and signals."

Consequently, (here comes the " Title" explanation) we need:

> To *discern* ("to decode"), what has been *burned into* our thought processes by the world spirit ("encoded"), so that the Holy Spirit of God may *restore* ("recoding"), the *Father's will and way* as the governing circuitry of our life and thought ("the first code").

The Bible puts it in these words:

> *And do not be conformed to this world, but be transformed by the renewing of your mind, that you may prove what is that good and acceptable and perfect will of God.*
> *Romans 12:2*

The *re*-conforming of our minds from the world's order of thinking is central to a man's finding his IMAGE in God again. Before we examine any of this process further, I want to be clear in our definition of "the world's image." The terminology itself can sound so petty and nitpicking: "the world's image" can sound like a puritanical, self-righteous, petty dart game waging an "Us vs. Them" or "The Churchy" versus "The Nasty" contest.

My concern about this clarity of definition is because as I was growing up, it seemed I heard the words "worldly" and "worldliness" in church constantly. This usually involved mentioning a list which included about a dozen *"don't do's."* So, generally, it was assumed if you *didn't* do those things, you were a "good Christian." It seemed much like a 4-year-old's "star chart," as when a child is being taught to, "Clean your fingernails (check), comb your hair (check), tie your own shoes (check)-- Hey, Gold Star!"

As adults, some believers have carried that mentality into the spiritual arena. They suppose that any "worldliness" or "world image" is outside the question if they have their "stars" for "not doing any of the bad things non-Christians do." But such legalistic propositions of righteousness are not the way of the Lord. The inner issues of the heart are far more significant than any list of "don't do's," for the heart is the source from which our actions spring. However, lest we smugly overlook "outside" issues, it would be reckless if you or I totally discounted the wisdom of personally watchdogging even those items on traditional lists of do's and don'ts. Because it *is* true that our habits, our appearance, and the ways we recreate and entertain ourselves DO reveal something of our heart attitudes to God's ways and will. So don't be too quick to trash "lists," because behind such legalism, you can still find something of a true *heart*-righteousness intended. Valid discernment was probably present at the inception of what may have now become a legalistic program.

But our focus on "world image" transcends any alienating, damning, separatist, or performance-oriented mind-set. Our quest for "A Man's Image and Identity" on God's terms has to do *not* with turning up the heat, twisting the screws, or making lists and condemning. We're seeking what the Incarnation of Jesus Christ *as a man* has opened for us; the door to, "*Christ in you, the hope of glory*" (Col. 1:27). His presence is the ultimate agent which can dissolve the world's image in us and imprint His.

Image, Imaging, Imagineering, Imagination.

They are more at the core of everything life contains than we probably perceive. From the *creation design* of "man in the image of God," to the *creative designs* of Madison Avenue's "image-making" of personalities and corporations for the purpose of mass-marketing, the concept of "image" surrounds us.

"Imaging" is the word often used to describe the impact of initial experiences upon our psyche. In short, when a specific encounter takes place, say between two people, the power of that encounter is such that it tends to set the grid over all future relationship, unless, of course, something changes the initial "imaging" impact of that encounter. This, for example, is why many men withdraw from either the *desire* to be a "spiritual man" or from the *belief* they could ever become so.

So often the "image" of what a "spiritual man" is has been shaped by encounters with fanatics on the one hand and godly giants on the other. To the first "image" the response is, "Not for me, no way, no how, if that nuttiness is what it means to be 'spiritual'!" To the second "image," usually seen in a spiritual leader whom the man respects, but who is so advanced in maturity and leadership the man feels a hopeless comparison, the response is passive. Most men would feel it was little use to even *think* of becoming so remarkable a person, and the positive "imaging" serves only to summon their respect because no relationship exists with the man to discover *how* such maturity or growth came about.

This brings us precisely to the heart of this study. I want to break in on the impact of any and every "image" that would hinder faith or that would obstruct growth. To do this I'm inviting you to join me in studying the idea of "image" as it is threaded throughout the Word of God. Some form of that word occurs about 200 times in the pages of Scripture. That doesn't include another 180+ times in which a form of the word "idol" occurs, and the two words must be fixed firmly in association if we're to think clearly about "A Man's Image and Identity." Idolatry--the substituting of an alternate image (or "circuit") for God's image (or intended purpose/plan/character) *in our lives--is* more of a fundamental problem than we often realize. So, let's look into the central concept of "image." Join me in an exciting survey.

First, I want to make a quick SIX-POINT TOUR of the Old Testament, and at each point post a principal issue concerning God's intended image for us as His own. So take your Bible in hand and prepare to mark these key points. And one other thing: Would you also prepare to think through each point--take ACTION, letting the Holy Spirit assist your meditation on each point's focus.

POINT 1: The Original Image--Gen. 1:26

> *Then God said, "Let Us make man in Our image, according to Our likeness; let them have dominion over the fish of the sea, over the birds of the air, and over the cattle, over all the earth and over every creeping thing that creeps on the earth."*

The Bible reveals our humanity to be the direct result of plan and purpose on the part of an almighty, all-knowing Creator. This contrasts sharply with the world-mind notion that man's existence is the chance result of primitive electro-chemical interactions at mankind's beginning, or that our personal being is only due to a chance sexual encounter by our own parents, bringing about our introduction to life as an individual. There is no way to exaggerate the importance of emphasizing the difference of these approaches, because everything spins in opposite directions from that juncture of understanding.

When the Bible says that we were made *"in the image of God,"* the matter of physical appearance is hardly in view. The essential element of sound-mindedness we're to gain from this revelation is that "in His image" means that God created us:

- With a capacity to relate to Him.
- With a potential for everlastingness.
- With a sovereign will of free, self-choice.
- With a mind to think and emotions to feel those thoughts and feelings which would produce actions that would profit us, fulfill our intended purpose, and rejoice both God's heart and ours.

The "Fall of Man"--the entry of sin into the race (Genesis 3)--damaged and twisted this image. With that, man's capacities and potentialities all remained intact. The problem was they all became *self*-centered rather than *God*-centered, and the now-blinded mind of man too entirely focuses on his own ego, and his soul too readily becomes a playground for demonic manipulation and extortion.

ACTION: Pause and review the original

"image" intent in the four statements above. What does each one mean to you, personally?

POINT 2: The Multiplied Defect--Gen. 5:3

> *And Adam lived one hundred and thirty years, and begot a son in his own likeness, after his image, and named him Seth.*

This may be the most tragic verse in the Bible. It reports the beginning of the *compounding* effect of sin now damaging the original image and intent of God for man. In direct terms the Scripture states that man, who had been made in GOD'S image, not only has fallen but is reproducing his offspring in HIS OWN image. In contrast to the earlier set of traits, when man was "in the image of God," we see each generation passing to the next these traits:

• A distancing from God, produced by fear and uncertainty.

• A lost view of "everlasting" values, replaced by a shortsighted view of "this moment" which prompts unwise urgency or wearying desperation.

• Free will, but one that makes choices motivated by a blinded mind and dulled, jaded emotions. Thus most choices are the product of a viewpoint--and image--being "sold" by the Arch-Deceiver, rather than from a clear-headed view of ultimate reality.

• The result is that whatever profit is gained or purpose fulfilled, it has limited-at-

43

best satisfaction, and God's intent is not only never realized--*it is not even perceived*!

The essential factors above are described in Ephesians 2:1-3. It's the status of all of us until God's grace rescues us and sets forward the process of redemption in our lives.

The crux of the "image" problem is in the fact that every one of us has been born with a scrambled "discerner," and we tend to not even recognize the world system's values being imprinted upon us. We become "conformed to the world image" by forfeit, and learn to think of distorted patterns of behavior and values as normal.

ACTION: List some matters in your own life that "seemed" normal, until the Holy Spirit pointed out to you the "world-image" in those practices. (Examples: How often we tolerate anger--"Dad was that way, so I guess it's normal that I am." We absorb prejudice and hatred--"I know I'm not perfect, but they're sure worse than I am and they deserve what they're getting." We learn socialized lying and dishonesty--"It wasn't really the truth, but it wasn't a lie that'd hurt anything"; or, "Those few stamps I used from the office aren't that big a deal, and besides, I stayed late last night and I didn't get anything for it.") Think this through. The matters brought to your mind may vary in apparent significance, but learning to let the Holy Spirit re-sensitize our inboard computer is key to our being

44

"re-imaged."

POINT 3: The Spreading Impact--Gen. 9:6

*Whoever sheds man's blood,
by man his blood shall be shed;
for in the image of God He
made man.*

It would be easy to pass by this refer-
ence to man's being made in the image of
God, presuming it to be only a divine decla-
ration concerning capital punishment. But
besides the fact that the rare and infinite
value of the human personality is asserted
by this edict of Heaven's Sovereign, the very
need for its being stated tells us something.
It forcibly brings to view the progressively
deteriorative power of the world image on
the human personality. In other words,
once the divine image is broken, things do
not stagnate at a "broken image" level, but
they grow worse. The whole context of this
verse displays this fact.

Murder was never approved by God, yet
when Cain slew Abel, God's mercy permit-
ted Cain to live (Genesis 4:1-15). But the
capacity of fallen flesh to further erode the
basic divine order, once the original image
has become distorted, is seen in Genesis
4:16-24. Here, Cain's offspring, Lamech,
not only kills in retaliation, but considers
himself to be a candidate for a reward for
having killed (vv. 23, 24). Genesis 6:11

further reveals how such violence spread. So the message is clear: The fallen image not only *replicates* itself, it *multiplies* and advances its capacity for evil and goes on to excuse its corruption. And so it was that following the Flood, God gave the command concerning capital punishment; not as a vendetta against murderers, but as a preventative against the fallen human drift toward violence and presumption and its lost perception on the value of life.

ACTION: Can you think of any example of how you tolerated one dimension of carnal indulgence, and later found it leading to an even deeper violation of God's values? What evidences are apparent that our society is characterized by this kind of fallen image impact? For example, have you found yourself becoming more passive toward our culture's casual or passive value on human life?

POINT 4: The Image-Making Prohibition--
Ex. 20:4; Lev. 26:1

> *You shall not make for yourself a carved image, or any likeness of anything that is in heaven above, or that is in the earth beneath, or that is in the water under the earth . . . You shall not make idols for yourselves; neither a carved image nor a sacred pillar shall*

*you rear up for yourselves; nor
shall you set up an engraved
stone in your land, to bow down
to it; for I am the Lord your God.*

It's amazing how applicable these commandments are today, especially remembering that almost every idol in the ancient world glorified either power or sensuality. These ancient "graven images" were far more than mere depictions of human beings. They were either (1) objects intended to summon the deification of human passions for power, prominence, or raw force; or (2) they were pornographic images designed to incite lust and motivate toward prostitution as a form of worship! But the awesome power of such images is not in the outward form, it is in the inner shaping that occurs in the personality. God's command was not merely some narrow-minded anti-artform or ban-the-statues cult. He was prohibiting His people's pursuit of surrounding themselves with things which engrave themselves on the psyche, which dehumanize and obliterate moral discernment.

ACTION: Have you ever found your inner mental speech habits impacted by exposure to profane language in the workplace or by films you've watched? Have you ever noticed that even if you didn't *speak* foul language, your mind revealed an imprint of its presence? What implications might this have on our thinking that we are supposedly immune to videos where we enjoy the comedy and pretend we are blanking out the profanity the script employs?

POINT 5: The Destruction Mandate--
         Deut. 7:1-11

> *When the Lord your God brings you into the land which you go to possess, and has cast out many nations before you . . . Thus you shall deal with them: you shall destroy their altars, and break down their sacred pillars, and cut down their wooden images, and burn their carved images with fire ...For you are a holy people to the Lord your God; the Lord your God has chosen you to be a people for Himself, a special treasure above all the peoples on the face of the earth.*

These few words from the longer passage of the Lord's command to Israel are as important to us today as to them when they entered the Canaanitish culture to conquer it. The "No Covenant--No Mercy" mandate (Deut. 7:2) sounds so brutal, we are tempted to rise in defense of those things before which God Almighty was so biting in His absolute commands. But a full reading of the text brings us to these words:

> *Therefore know that the Lord your God, He is God, the faithful God who keeps covenant and mercy for a thousand generations with those who love Him and keep His commandments.*

Let us be strongly reminded that God's call to destroy the images which His people encountered was motivated by His knowledge that if they didn't, those images would eventually destroy them!! Hear it, please: God's "No mercy" clause is an expression of His mercifulness! And when we grasp that, we'll understand all the more what horrific impact there is in the world's image system. Such idolatry--i.e., mind/habit control through "images"--can take any number of forms.

Ed was a football hero whose scrapbook recorded his exploits as a national sports figure. As a Christian he was faithful in his stand for Christ, a position he never reverted from--he was a good witness! But a strange thing happened.

At a time of weakness and weariness, he fell into a moral slippage which nearly cost him his marriage and his job. As he repented, the Holy Spirit directed him to burn his scrapbook. Ed later tells how the literal "images" of his accomplishments, reported and depicted on the news clippings, had preserved the notion of his being a "sports jock." So it was, when he was in a time of weakness due to worthy labor and other involvements including serving publicly the cause of Christ, a "hook" in the old image of himself drew him to a place of unwittingly trying to prove "I still have the old stuff," and it led to the edge of moral destruction.

ACTION: While Ed's experience doesn't require a legalistic response that everyone burn their memorabilia, it's amazing how frequently our attics hold mementoes that prompt memories that tug us toward repeating past failures. Where in your life do you need to allow God's Spirit to deal with such matters and to mold you into one who resists *any* facet of the world image?

POINT 6: The Self-Defined Image--
                 Judg. 17, 18

> *In those days the tribe of the Danites was seeking an inheritance for itself . . .*

The entire book of Judges is a disgraceful display of the lengths to which even God's own people may revert in unworthy ways when a clear vision of GOD'S IMAGE is lost to their eyes. (We'll see later that there *is* a revealed "image of God.") The brief text above is taken from the center of a two-chapter passage that involves a man named Micah, who isn't to be confused with the prophet whose book bears his name. There's a powerful warning in this extended portion of the Bible: It's a warning about the potential death-dealing force of self-defined religion--what happens when a person *thinks* he's tapped into God via some privileged pathway, even though it's a path God prohibits to everyone else.

The more memorable cases--such as Jim Jones and the Guyana tragedy--are usually supposed to exhaust the way this deception occurs. But Micah's cultivating *his own image* and then calling it God, can happen as quickly in the secret recesses of an individual soul as in a group which is destroyed as it mindlessly follows a religious madman.

Note that not only was Micah deluded by his self-developed image, but he also became the instrument for leading a whole tribe of Israel into idolatrous confusion. Their vulnerability is hinted at in words which might be spoken about many people you and I meet *and influence* today: "They were seeking their own inheritance."

I have to listen carefully here, for it's a solemn reminder that if I fall into defining my own ways and standards as "the image of correctness," there are many who are seeking *something* and may settle for what I represent, however false my example or leadership.

ACTION: Let's ask these questions: Even if the example I present is right, is it

51

possible that personal pride in my example could poison its spiritual power potential? What is self-righteousness, and how does Micah's case represent its destructive power? Dad, what does your church attendance pattern model to your kids--all week long? In what way might a well-intended man pollute his potential for good by creating his own standard of discipleship as a substitute for God's?

This study of the Old Testament's development of the idea of "images" traverses the span from God's image to man's self-constructed substitute. We've seen:

• The original image FOR MAN as God conferred it upon him.

• The fallen and multiplied image OF MAN as sin relays it.

• The reminder how images THROUGH MAN become further debased.

• The command of God TO MAN to give no place to world-images.

• The instruction of God THAT MAN destroy world images in his possession.

• The warning from God as to HOW MAN can delude himself by self-contrived images.

Perhaps this study would merit recurrent review or conversational interaction with another brother in Christ. The lessons don't end here, nor does the biblical revelation of human folly generated by world-images conclude with these few key examples.

As we've earlier observed: With the subject of images, we're at the core of our call to be men of discernment who know WHAT we're about, HOW we're being shaped, and WHO we are.

Where do we go from here?

Chapter Four
TRANSFORMED INTO HIS IMAGE

It was a disgusting revelation of my own inner smallness. It surfaced a horrible flaw in my sense of security and confidence in my person--my identity. I failed at both points: (1) feeling threatened by a comparison with another man's achievement, and (2) feeling submerged by his apparent excellence when statistics showed his work exceeded the fruit of my efforts. Let me tell you about it.

It began with a tour of a new church facility. You would think I would be thrilled: "Look, God's Kingdom advancing!" But not so--at least, not *that* day! For the further I went as I was being led by our host, the more I found myself fighting to be honestly *glad.* After all, this man was in the same vocation as I, and the expansive, marvelously developed, brand-new-church-campus was vastly more beautiful and grand than where I serve.

I labored to quench the detestable surge of the spirits of comparison and competition--they're ferocious when those demons assail a man's identity! I thought I might be winning over the temptations, until we turned a corner and entered the area where the tapes of this pastor's messages were duplicated and shipped to all parts of the world. Granting myself the carnality of inquiring, "How many tapes are shipped each month?" (privately and sinfully hoping it was fewer than the number distributed of mine), I was suddenly sorry I'd asked. The numbers were astronomical by comparison with mine. I winced inwardly, and minutes later almost slinked away. When I might have rejoiced in the gifting of a dear man of God, when I might have praised the Lord for the marvelous evidence of divine grace bringing about tremendous fruit, I was tinged by jealousy and ashamed before the Holy Spirit's convicting me of such pitiful smallness of soul.

Please answer me, Sir. Do you recognize *anything* of yourself in my sad response?

I'm happy to say I wasted little time in repenting that day, but the fact I felt such intimidation, such erosion of my own identity, is due to an *image* problem--resulting in an *identity* crisis. You see, brother, at the root of my failure was a two-step mistake:

1. Yielding to comparison, I was looking at the IMAGE OF MAN, rather than seeing the IMAGE OF GOD in the creative uniqueness of God's grace in him. In effect, I was making myself an enemy of the Creator by beginning to resent what He had done through my fellow-pastor friend.

2. Yielding to competition, I was bowing to the IMAGE OF A MAN's accomplishment, rather than rejoicing in the IMAGE OF GOD's mightiness at work in powerful productiv-

ity. In doing so, I put myself in competition with God's sovereign choice and divine almightiness. How senseless and stupid! To attempt competing with God is to name yourself a loser in advance!

I ended up winning that day--winning because I returned my identity to its proper place: in Jesus Christ my Lord. And I confessed my sin of becoming so wrapped up in the IMAGE OF A MAN that I missed worshiping the manifest evidence of GOD HIMSELF at work in a wonderful way. The *quick* transformation came about because the *truth* of God's transforming my mind had found a place long before, even though the place of that truth in practical application suffered a momentary lapse that day.

Let's pursue this great truth of "transformation into Christ's image" as it unfolds in the New Testament.

The Image Of God

Jesus came not only to save mankind's *eternity* from destruction, but He also came to save mankind's *identity* from confusion. In His sinless life and death we are provided with forgiveness of sin and given the hope of heaven. But in His matchless person and nature we see the revelation of all that man-the-creature was meant to be. And we are provided with a hope--"the hope of glory"--by the promise that this matchless One has not only come *to* us to save, but is ready to dwell *in* us, to bring life:

*   *Life* with a sense of destiny, bringing *confidence*;
*   *Life* with a sense of adequacy, bringing *joy*;
*   *Life* with a sense of His abiding, overthrowing *fear*,

. . . *Confidence* that walks without a strut and doesn't need to prove itself.

. . . *Joy* that lives with a satisfaction in God's sufficiency, removed from the carnal need to prove oneself equal to anyone.

. . . *Fear* that is overthrown, giving pride no place to gain a footing, for pride is only the false constructions pushed into position to compensate for whatever we fear "isn't enough" in ourselves.

Brother, pause to think on these things because the starting place for our securing a continual sense of adequacy, confidence, and fearlessness is to not only *see* God's image in Jesus, but to experience our being *transformed* into that same image. Look at the Scriptures with me.

Just as the Old Testament Scriptures reveal God's original image and plan for us, and describe the sorry process of deterioration that occurred by reason of man's pursuit of false images, the New Testament opens with hope. Defining that hope is seldom done in a thorough way.

Usually, the Gospel is summarized in a "get-saved-and-go-to-heaven-some-day" statement, which is true as far as it goes, but it leapfrogs right over the powerful *present* purposes of God in a man's life. *Besides* our receiving forgiveness of sins and the promise of eternity in heaven through our Lord Jesus Christ, we are *also* promised:

1. The daily enablement of the Holy Spirit for every practical detail of our life and living.

2. The wisdom of God for growth in our marriage, raising our kids, and conducting business on our jobs.

3. The increase of God's grace deepening into the fabric of our nature and strengthening our character.

4. The provision of God's promises for our physical strength and health, and our material and financial blessing.

5. The unlimited power of prayer to avenue through us by the Holy Spirit's power and to impact and change circumstances in the world around us.

While this summary doesn't elaborate all the abundance promised us in the *here and now*, it's enough to incite any thinking man's question: "How can I grow in this order of living?" And the answer is, *"Christ in you, the hope of glory"* (Col. 1:27). A THREE-POINT trip through key New Testament scriptures shows why--and *how*!

NEW TESTAMENT STEP ONE:
The Penetration

And the Word became flesh
and dwelt among us, and we

beheld His glory, the glory as of the only begotten of the Father, full of grace and truth. No one has seen God at any time. The only begotten Son, who is in the bosom of the Father, He has declared Him.

John 1:14, 18

Because mankind had a dual need, God became flesh to address *both*--the need of a REDEEMER and the need of a RESTORER.

As *Redeemer*, Jesus became one of us because His *death*, as a human being, was a legal requirement of God's justice. There is no other Way (John 14:6) and there is no other Person (Acts 4:12) by which this could be done.

As *Restorer*, however, Jesus became one of us because His *life*, as a human being, provided a spiritual demonstration of God's ability to reinstate His image in human flesh. In other words, God not only makes a way to *save* mankind, but He also reveals His plan to repenetrate mankind with His image.

That's the reason the Scriptures are so meticulously clear on this point: Jesus was the Image of God *as* a man to reveal that image again, *among* mankind to display that image again, and *unto* mankind to offer that image again!

Read these thoughtfully:

- **God's glory (image) is promised to "all flesh."**

> The glory of the Lord shall be
> revealed, and all flesh shall
> see it together; for the mouth
> of the Lord has spoken.
> *Isaiah 40:5*

- **God's glory becomes incarnate in His Son, Jesus.**

> And the Word became flesh
> and dwelt among us, and we
> beheld His glory, the glory as
> of the only begotten of the
> Father, full of grace and truth.
> *John 1:14*

- **God's Person (image/character) is displayed in Jesus.**

> He who has seen Me has seen
> the Father . . . The words that
> I speak to you I do not speak
> on My own authority; but the
> Father who dwells in Me does
> the works.   *John 14:9, 10*

- **Satan fights this reentry of God's revealed image.**

> . . . The god of this age has
> blinded (the minds of those)
> who do not believe, lest the

> *light of the gospel of the glory*
> *of Christ, who is the image of*
> *God, should shine on them.*
> *2 Corinthians 4:4*

• As the "repenetrating" image of God to mankind, Jesus Christ is called "the firstborn"--that is, the beginning point of a new race of the Redeemed.

> *He is the image of the invisible*
> *God, the firstborn over all cre-*
> *ation.*   *Colossians 1:15*

• Now, our Savior--the Redeeming Man who has come to be the Restoring Man--is enthroned. He has initiated the path of God's desire for all who are saved--to remake the image of God in us, and to restore us to the high destiny intended in our creation.

> *Who being the brightness of*
> *His glory and the express im-*
> *age of His person, and uphold-*
> *ing all things by the word of*
> *His power, when He had by*
> *Himself purged our sins, sat*
> *down at the right hand of the*
> *Majesty on high . . . For it was*
> *fitting for Him, for whom are all*
> *things and by whom are all*
> *things, in bringing many sons*
> *to glory, to make the author of*
> *their salvation perfect through*

sufferings.
Hebrews 1:3; 2:10

The summary testimony of these texts is that God's plan to *redeem* man included more than recovering from sin and death. God's purpose is to reinstate His image in each of us--to recreate *in* us the very thing which will complete our intended being: *both* to KNOW God and to SHOW His Person and Presence through our lives by reason of His fullness indwelling us.

NEW TESTAMENT STEP TWO:
The Transformation

The beauty of the Gospel plan for our experiencing God's image restored in us is that the same grace that *re-penetrated* is poured out to us by the Holy Spirit to see that image *reinstated* too! Look at these clear-cut statements of that expectation offered to us:

• Paul prayed for this image to be formed in people.

> *My little children, for whom I labor in birth again until Christ is formed in you.*
> *Galatians 4:19*

• God is totally committed to seeing His image in us again.

> *For whom He foreknew, He*

> *also predestined to be con-*
> *formed to the image of His Son,*
> *that He might be the firstborn*
> *among many brethren.*
> *Romans 8:29*

- **Our walk and worship of Christ pave the way to this.**

> *I beseech you therefore, breth-*
> *ren, by the mercies of God, that*
> *you present your bodies a liv-*
> *ing sacrifice, holy, acceptable*
> *to God, which is your reason-*
> *able service* (literally, 'your spiritual worship'). *And do*
> *not be conformed to this world,*
> *but be transformed by the re-*
> *newing of your mind, that you*
> *may prove what is the good*
> *and acceptable and perfect will*
> *of God.* *Romans 12:1, 2*

The evidence is there and the promise is contained within it. Dear brother of mine, we're offered the chance for a reinstatement of God's image in each of us. What a towering possibility! What a removal from the relentless "push" to establish our own status, verify our own worth, build our own image, secure our own identities!!

If it could happen, it would (1) break the human desperation to "be someone," for God's dwelling within us in fullness would cause us to be satisfied that we ARE complete in Him.

> *For in Him dwells all the fullness of the Godhead bodily, and you are complete in Him who is the head of all principality and power.* Col. 2:9, 10

If it could happen, it would (2) break the human pattern of sin, with its manifold expressions of anger, lust, dishonesty, and coveting, for God's dwelling within us in fullness would remove the insatiable quest to "have things" or "control things."

> *Therefore, let no one glory in men, for all things are yours ...the world or life or death, or things present or things to come--all are yours. And you are Christ's and Christ is God's.* 1 Cor. 3:21-23

> *But seek the kingdom of God, and all these things shall be added to you. Do not fear, little flock, for it is your Father's good pleasure to give you the kingdom.* Luke 12:31, 32

And the glorious part of God's program of rescuing and restoring mankind is that it CAN happen: God's image CAN be restored in us. And here's how.

*NOW THE LORD IS THE SPIRIT;
AND WHERE THE SPIRIT OF
THE LORD IS, THERE IS LIB-
ERTY. BUT WE ALL WITH UN-
VEILED FACE* (i.e., fully open
to His work in us) *BEHOLDING
AS IN A MIRROR* (i.e., God's
Word) *THE GLORY OF THE
LORD* (i.e., Jesus' fullness,
character, and revelation of
the Father's image), *ARE BE-
ING TRANSFORMED INTO THE
SAME IMAGE FROM GLORY
TO GLORY, JUST AS BY THE
SPIRIT OF THE LORD.*
2 Cor. 3:17,18

Would you join me, Sir? Let's rise for a moment in praise to the wisdom and grace of the Living God! For with these texts and in this truth we are being told, "Your identity problems, your image-making quests, can be put to rest if you'll hear Me!" God has given His Son and sent His Spirit--to *recover* and *reinstate* us and to so *fully reveal His image in us*--that we are given His "hope of glory!"

• Hope that the "glory" of His presence will grow His purpose in us as we give place to His Spirit;

• Hope that every vestige of carnal surrender to fear, lust, or pride can eventually be removed from our life-patterns;

• Hope that the depth of Christ's work

in our lives will evaporate the need for self-verification, as He verifies His work in and through us.

• Hope that "Christ in you" will crowd out all smallness and pettiness and wrestling with human comparisons and competitiveness--for *now* our manhood is secured in His!

The Obvious Question: How Now?

The promise of "Christ in you" is to be received. But it's a promise we begin to *live out*, not an electric switch we *turn on*. The confession I made at the beginning of this chapter--my struggle with smallness when visiting another church site--is the reminder that we're called to a *growth* program, not an *instant-action* one. My temptation to regression was overcome quickly. But that quick comeback was a different thing from earlier traits of (1) not being aware at all of my entrapment in self-image making (during earlier years of my experience); and (2) my beginning lessons at confronting such temptations to smallness or false masculinity (which I didn't overcome quickly--and at previous times I stumbled completely). But if I've learned any lessons, they are these:

FIRST: Believe in the *promise* of the Holy Spirit to restore God's image in you.

SECOND: Receive the *power* of the Holy Spirit to fill you daily, enabling obedience and faith as you walk with Jesus.

THIRD: Respond to the *presence* of the Holy Spirit when He speaks, giving instruction or correction at points where *your* image-making or struggle with identity may be occurring.

FOURTH: Rest in the *process* of the Holy Spirit's indwelling. He isn't going to go away!! He's come to abide, and as long as you remain committed to the first three points, the fourth will assure His fulfillment of the word--

"CHRIST IN YOU . . . THE HOPE OF GLORY!"

Early in this chapter I said there are three New Testament Steps in the "transformation process" bringing us back into the image of the Creator through our Redeemer Jesus Christ. I've intentionally left the third step as a P.S. to this book. You'll find it later on page 77.

Chapter Five
CIRCUMCISION:
THE SEAL OF HIS IMAGE

There is only one way for us to fully enter into the Lord's design for us as men: Circumcision . . .

The *circumcision* of our *hearts*!

There is probably no more masculine image in the Bible than the powerfully pictured truth typified in the ancient rite of circumcision--the surgical removal of the excess flesh from the foreskin of the male sex organ. But the New Testament applies this to the *heart* of a man, and thereby we're introduced to a dynamic truth.

It began with Abraham and the covenant that released his promised life-begetting capacity (Gen. 17). Then the covenant was transmitted to successive generations, as the Lord proscribed to the nation of Israel that they circumcise every male on the eighth day.

I want you to see with me how this was the Lord's mark, an *image*, that He placed on His people. For example, with the application of this image in Joshua's time, God said, "I have rolled away the reproach of Egypt from off you." Point: You're no longer bound by the slave-image of your past, but you're now cut loose to the promise of your future! "The reproach of Egypt" is a figure of speech that speaks to us about the image of this world, and as such it represents many things:

- Patterns of the past dictating the present.
- World-worship and materialistic pursuit.
- Intimidation, fear, and carnal competitiveness.
- Conformity to compromising expectations.
- Being trapped or leashed to empty tradition.
- The pressure to perform to verify worth.
- Self-concepts of limitation and restriction.

. . . All rolled away--rolled away because the Lord is instituting a new economy of things. It's not the Lord supplying us with more carnal currency to attempt buying into the world's vain "economy" of values. Rather, He gives us a new economy--a new sense of Kingdom worth. It's a real and exceeding wealth which is based on an economy rooted in the spiritual currency of Christ's work on the Cross; an economy driven by the quickening of the Holy Spirit inside us. His transforming power within you and me has enormous purchasing ability; buying us a new life-power that's *first* born *in* us, and *then* can be cut loose *through* us.

The image of circumcision is powerfully instructive, because it depicts a man's call to let God determine which image will mark him.

In Genesis 17, the Lord first calls Abraham to receive circumcision as a mark and seal of the covenant.

> *And he received the sign of circumcision, a seal of the righteousness of the faith which he had while still uncircumcised, that he might be the father of all those who believe, though they are uncircumcised, that righteousness might be imputed to them also.*   Romans 4:11

Have you ever wondered how Abraham might have responded when the Lord told him this was to be the seal of his agreement with Him? It must have been startling! To begin, it was a new practice. And further, it not only was a sensitive subject by reason of the anatomy involved, but the world around thought the Jews foolish for circumcising themselves, and they were mocked by the rest of society as "body-mutilators."

The world will always mock the image God designs for a man. (In the case of physical circumcision, it's only been in this century that the practice has received confirmation from the medical community as to its value in personal hygiene. But until now, the Jewish community bore the brunt of scorn because they were not of the same image--the world's.)

Circumcision does come with a price. The physical rite teaches spiritual lessons in a very personal way.

First, in circumcision there is no recourse to privacy. The mechanics of the surgery involve *exposure*. Spiritually applied, our circumcision of the heart involves our allowing--indeed, welcoming--God to deal with our hearts; willingly exposing to Him the private matters of our soul. While there are no secrets unknown to Him, there are places where He knows surgery is essential to imprint His image on us, but upon which He will not work without our trust and submission. Thus, the circumcised heart admits that there is no private reserve withheld from God. Openness before Him--a nakedness of soul--keeps everything exposed. We stand as *His* alone; in the blaze of His presence daily.

Second, in physical circumcision there is no escape from pain. The process cuts. In the book of Joshua we read that it took three days for the men to recover from the pain of circumcision when administered in adult years rather than early in life as intended. This isn't some form of spiritual masochism. It's simply dealing with things that should have been dealt with sooner--yielding to the application of God's Word as the Spirit's sword, in circumcising action, slices away the surplus, the unnecessary, the excess. Flesh is pared that God's glory might be revealed in us--a new identity. And *identity* is the central issue, for *thirdly*--

Circumcision cuts to the core of a man's identity.

The physical act of circumcision impacts that very member identifying a man's manhood. "It's a boy," was one day proclaimed, and this physical member provided identity. Now God cuts away at the heart of a man's false quests for recognition, shallow programs of ego-centeredness, every self-dependent enterprise at securing my own identity. And it's all that God Himself might declare of you--of me: "It's a *man* now!"

The benefits of circumcision impact a lifetime . . . and an eternity.

> *In Him you were also circumcised with the circumcision made without hands, by putting off the body of the sins of the flesh, by the circumcision of Christ, buried with Him in baptism, in which you also were raised with Him through faith in the working of God, who raised Him from the dead.*
> *Col. 2:11-12*

. . . Resurrection power and a changed life replace the momentary pain of circumcision.

Circumcision of the heart affects specific outworkings; manifestations of God's paring back the superficial. By this inner process of circumcision, He can bring us to our true identity in Him.

Remember years back when long hair and beards gained stylish acceptance? It was in that context that my friend, Jerry Cook, a fellow-pastor, told of a young man in his church who was a dedicated partner in ministry. Buck genuinely loved working with the young people in Jerry's congregation and he had a strong love for Jesus. He also happened to have very long hair and a beard. The latter is what occasioned Buck's becoming a tender illustration regarding "image" and a man's "identity."

One day, as Buck was walking downtown, he passed by the local barber shop. He later admitted that as he did, a kind of sneer rose up within him; smirking to himself, "Man, nobody's *ever* going to get me into a place like that! Thank you, Lord, I'm a *free spirit*, unbound by anybody's social conventions!" But almost instantly the Holy Spirit pierced his soul. The Heavenly Voice whispered, "Buck, are you willing to get your hair cut?"

"Lord, you know I don't need to do that! No way! I'm free!"

And it was then--then and there--that the Lord stopped him in his tracks: "Buck, you *could* have kept your hair long. But now, because you said, 'No,' I'm calling you to do it. Get a haircut, and do it now." And the holy punchline completed Buck's own testimony of this circumcising encounter: "Buck, I'm asking you to get your hair cut because *the roots of your hair have grown into your heart.*"

The incident thunders with practical insight and revelation. God wasn't mocking the man, He was being *merciful* to him. He was identifying a point in a man where his identity was confused with "image," and where the *real* man needed to be redefined. It involved circumcision--God touching a point where Buck's fruitfulness in ministering to others was in jeopardy because he could no longer distinguish between the value and sufficiency of Christ's image in him and the empty value of wearing a costume of individuality.

Whenever my liberty begins to become a pridefully-carried thing, I'm in danger. When I replace God's values with my own situational ethics, I'm in trouble. If I see in myself an insistence for my own way; if I rationalize it and tell God, "it's okay because I still love You"--even though I'm not meeting Him eye-to-eye and heart-to-heart--then I'm trading my real identity for a false one.

Please understand me. I'm not talking about *hair.* I'm talking about *heart.* Buck's hair was a part of his past values--values now in transition. A new identity was now being unfolded in Christ. However, a residue of false-identification with the world's image remained and needed to be addressed by God. It's at that point when God confronts us with the need to let Him change our image that our decision needs to be made.

A heart-check is in progress.

And the image into which we have allowed our hearts to be molded into over the years and months--whether it is the computer-chip circuit of the Holy Spirit's creation or the circuit design of this world--will yield a decision compatible with that image.

Until the Lord starts doing a work in the heart, the exterior elements have little significance. But as soon as He points something out to you or me, then we become responsible. Matters may be tolerated by reason of our own immaturity or deafness of soul--until *now*. Then, the Lord will speak to us about forms of habit; about attitudes; about things we eat, drink, listen to, watch--and how much. But He *never, ever* does this to diminish our pleasure or joy. The Bible says, "At your right hand there are pleasures forever more," and Jesus said, "I came that men might have life and have it more *abundantly.*" And that will always be the consequence of heart circumcision: greater joy--greater abundance of grace in our lives. He shapes us as a tree is pruned so that *the fruit will increase*, not so our potential will wither up and die.

Listen please, Sir. You can:

. . . be saved and be filled with His Spirit;

. . . pray for hours daily and win souls to Christ;

. . . touch lives, give to the poor, fast consistently; and

. . . love people, serve greatly, and even give time to the PTA.

But all the while the Lord may be saying to you, "There's this *place* in your heart where I need to shape My image--through surgery." The most mature among us will periodically find new areas where the Father wants to reshape, refine, or renew His image in us. So never cease that availability to His ongoing transformation. It's the pathway to fruitfulness, dear brother. And it's the path to gaining an unshakeable certainty of who He is. And who you are.

PS: A Final Word . . .
OUR ULTIMATE HOPE

It's been a happy task to walk beside you, my brother.

These pages, directed toward pursuing the pathway of our growth, as men who care about God's way, as we seek a way past "world-image" entrapment, self-security, and false-identity systems, has been a pleasure to pursue. I hope it's been that for you, too.

But I didn't want to conclude without inviting you to look *beyond* the present; to look to the ultimate tomorrow, and the Coming of our Lord Jesus Christ.

It's not only good to keep His Return on our mind as a daily point of joyful expectation, but there are also wonderful references to His Coming which bear on our subject of God's image in us.

NEW TESTAMENT STEP THREE: The Ultimate Transformation

In Chapter Four, I state there are three New Testament Steps to a man's full transformation into the image of God. Then, I concluded the chapter by saying I would not deal with the last one until this closing note in our study.

My reason for waiting is my awareness that too many believers put so much anticipation in the Return of Jesus as the answer to every personal or earthly dilemma, that they don't bother to give attention to their own responsibility for growth in Him *now*--before His Coming.

Though we have studied the massive potential of "Christ in you--the hope of glory--NOW!", I still don't want to sign-off without pointing you toward a high promise in God's Word which lifts our eyes to the glorious hope of Jesus' Return; to the *ultimate transformation we'll experience.*

Whatever we realize of God's restored image in us during this lifetime--and there's *much* awaiting us--let's make no mistake; the *consummate* transformation will occur when Jesus appears to receive His people unto Himself:

> *Beloved, now we are children of God; and it has not yet been revealed what we shall be, but we know that when He is revealed, we shall be like Him, for we shall see Him as He is. And everyone who has this hope in Him purifies himself, just as He is pure.*
> *1 John 3:2-3*

Please notice the wisdom in the tension this text keeps before us. It's the very truth that has prompted my leaving this part of our study for now.

The Apostle John writes to say, "There's a GREAT transformation coming--WE WILL BE LIKE HIM--EXACTLY AND COMPLETELY!" But then he adds, "If you have this hope, then expect the refining, renewing ('purifying') process to be operational *now.*"

This same concept is presented in the Apostle Paul's letter to the Corinthians:

> *And as we have borne the image of the man of dust, we shall also bear the image of the heavenly Man.*
> 1 Cor. 15:49

The surrounding text points to the ultimate day of our Lord when, at His Return, all the residue of human corruptibility and mortality will be *transcended* by the glory of our *translation* (the Rapture); and we'll be *transformed* totally--completely and eternally changed to enter eternity with our Savior.

There's not a man alive who has the slightest notion as to what the eternal future holds for us. But we can count on this: It's something worthy of God's creativity! Don't lock heaven down to the size of our tiny minds. It'll be more than a long-term vacation, more than an eternal retirement home, more than an endless party.

God created us in His image because He has imagined timeless wonders for our enjoyment with and beside Him, forever. So now that salvation has brought us back on track toward that destiny, let's grow in our true identity, as His present grace *progresses* the reinstatement of His image in us. And then, Sir--

Keep your eyes heavenward, for the day of our consummate and final transformation is near. Join me in:

> *Looking for that blessed hope*
> *and glorious appearing of our*
> *great God and Savior Jesus*
> *Christ.*　　　　*Titus 2:13*

Let's keep growing in Him until then, brother. And though you and I may never meet until that Day, I'll see you there.

With Him.

DEVOTIONS

IN THE LAST EIGHT CHAPTERS OF

ROMANS

Contributed by Bob Anderson

The second half of the Book of Romans divides up into five main topical sections:

- Issues regarding God and Israel are discussed in 9:1-11:36;
- Rich applications of the Christian life are supplied to us in 12:1-15:13;
- Paul talks about his own ministry and plans in 15:14-33;
- Paul's personal greetings are found in 16:1-24; and,
- Paul gives his personal benediction in 16:25-27.

In the majority of these verses (12:1-15:13) Paul deals with the issue of Christian conduct, i.e., how we should live out our faith. He stresses that spirituality should be concretely expressed and evidenced by our actions in daily life.

(It is suggested that this devotional be used for stimulating discussion and prayer within a small group of men meeting regularly.)

☐ **Today's Text: Romans 9:1-5** *(key v. 3)*

1 Today's Truth: Here is a staggering display of compassion on Paul's part toward his countrymen. His love for them was so great that he was willing, if it were possible, to be condemned to hell himself if somehow it might provide salvation for the Jews. Of course, such an ambition is impossible, but the heart of the Savior is seen in Paul.

Today's Thoughts: _____

_____

_____

☐ **Today's Text: Romans 9:6-13** *(key v.8)*

2 Today's Truth: The outward image of being a Jew doesn't ultimately profit a man in God's Kingdom. It is the internal image being born of faith that makes one a "child of the promise"--one who is a Jew *inwardly* (Rom. 2:29).

Today's Thoughts: _____

_____

_____

☐ **Today's Text: Romans 9:14-19** *(key v. 18)*

3 Today's Truth: This verse doesn't mean that God prevents the unsaved from believing. It means that God uses both mercy and wrath to accomplish His redemptive purposes, and His heart does not desire *anyone* to perish.

Today's Thoughts: _____

_____

_____

☐ **Today's Text: Romans 9:20-26** *(key v. 22)*

4 **Today's Truth:** "What about God making people vessels of wrath!--*that's* not fair!" But the old saying is true: "the same sun that melts wax, hardens clay." God's miracles performed right under Pharoah's nose couldn't soften him because of his predisposition to hardness. So God used Pharoah's rebellion to show His glorious might.

Today's Thoughts: ————————————

————————————————————————

————————————————————————

☐ **Today's Text: Romans 9:27-33** *(key v.29)*

5 **Today's Truth:** "Unless the Lord of Hosts had left us a *seed*, we would have become like Sodom"! God's DNA, the image-making power of Christ in us, preserves us from the moral decay and degradation of our Adamic sin nature.

Today's Thoughts: ————————————

————————————————————————

☐ **Today's Text: Romans 10:1-10** *(key v. 9)*

6 **Today's Truth:** How sweet and simple the knowledge of eternal salvation is! Paul could not have said it more succinctly than he did in verse 9.

Today's Thoughts: ————————————

————————————————————————

————————————————————————

☐ **Today's Text: Romans 10:11-15** *(key v. 14)*

7 **Today's Truth:** There are times when a silent witness is important--when people can *see* Christ in us instead of just get an earful of words. But ultimately, salvation only comes through *hearing* and responding to the Gospel.

Today's Thoughts: _____

_____

_____

☐ **Today's Text: Romans 10:16-21** *(key v.16)*

8 **Today's Truth:** Israel cannot plead ignorance of the Good News or charge that God has been unfair with them--for they *refused* to believe the Gospel, though they were the first to hear it.

Today's Thoughts: _____

_____

_____

☐ **Today's Text: Romans 11:1-8** *(key v. 7)*

9 **Today's Truth:** The majority of the nation of Israel became blinded to the Gospel. The Greek word means that they literally had become callous or petrified against the truth. But verse 8 says "*God* has given them . . . eyes that they should not see." Why? Because that's what *they* had chosen. God simply induced a catalyst to speed up the process of manifesting *their own choice*.

Today's Thoughts: _____

_____

_____

☐ **Today's Text: Romans 11:9-14** *(key v. 14)*

10 **Today's Truth:** God's rejection of Israel is not final. For it is God's desire that the Jews eventually become jealous of the Gentiles' relationship with Christ, and thereby believe in the Gospel.

Today's Thoughts: ⸺

⸺

⸺

☐ **Today's Text: Romans 11:15-21** *(key v.18)*

11 **Today's Truth:** The human tendency toward racism and/or spiritual pride is addressed here. Paul reminds us that we must never forget that salvation is from the Jews.

Today's Thoughts: ⸺

⸺

⸺

☐ **Today's Text: Romans 11:22-29** *(key v. 26)*

12 **Today's Truth:** Paul is not saying that every Jewish person who ever lived will be saved. He is speaking in the collective sense, meaning that there will be a massive turning of the Jews to faith in Christ at some point in the future.

Today's Thoughts: ⸺

⸺

⸺

☐ **Today's Text: Romans 11:30-36** *(key v. 32)*

13 Today's Truth: Paul is touching on one of those truths that is extremely deep for the human mind. God began with the Jews, but included an era for the Gentiles, and then will soon embrace the Jews once more. And by this, He is doing everything possible to save as many people as possible throughout all of history, even though His dealings may appear, at times, to be quite severe.

Today's Thoughts: _____

_____

_____

☐ **Today's Text: Romans 12:1-5** *(key v.2)*

14 Today's Truth: We are not to be *conformed* to this world. The Greek word for *conformed* is *suschematizo*. Recognize the word "schematic"–as in blueprints for an electronic circuit? We must not let our "circuitry" be programmed by this world's system of values.

Today's Thoughts: _____

_____

_____

☐ **Today's Text: Romans 12:6-13** *(key v. 6)*

15 Today's Truth: Paul stresses that we should use the gifts God has given us. Have you asked God to show you your spiritual gifts and how to use them?

Today's Thoughts: _____

_____

_____

☐ **Today's Text: Romans 12:14-21** *(key v. 17)*

16 Today's Truth: Verse 17 is one of a myriad of verses in Scripture defining in exact terms what the outworkings of the image of Christ are to be in our lives. "Repay no one evil for evil"–that certainly is contrary to the image of this world!

Today's Thoughts: _____

_____

_____

☐ **Today's Text: Romans 13:1-7** *(key v. 1)*

17 Today's Truth: "Oh no! Being conformed to the image of Christ relates to how honestly I pay my taxes? Does God really care about 1040s and 1099s? I mean, the Government is corrupt! I deserve to–" . . . Verse 7 tells us God's reply.

Today's Thoughts: _____

_____

_____

 Today's Text: Romans 13:8-14 *(key v.14)*

18 Today's Truth: If any one of us "makes provision" for our flesh, something of corruption–in one form or another–will grow. To "make provision for" means to "plan ahead or make preparation for" gratifying the carnal nature; not stumbling into sin, but premeditated action.

Today's Thoughts: _____

_____

_____

☐ **Today's Text: Romans 14:1-6** *(key v. 1)*

19 **Today's Truth:** The image of Christ in us will cause us to put loving receptivity towards a brother or sister above debate and striving to be right about non-essential issues, i.e., those things which are neither commanded nor forbidden in the Word.

Today's Thoughts: _____

_____

_____

☐ **Today's Text: Romans 14:7-13** *(key v.10)*

20 **Today's Truth:** Paul mentions that we will all stand before the Judgment Seat of Christ. He presents this as a motivator so that we will love one another without contempt. This is not a threat of hell--the Judgment Seat of Christ determines the believer's rewards in heaven, not his salvation.

Today's Thoughts: _____

_____

_____

☐ **Today's Text: Romans 14:14-23** *(key v. 19)*

21 **Today's Truth:** When tempted to argue with a loved one over a petty issue, remember verse 19: "Pursue things which make for peace." We are to actively seek ways we might build up others.

Today's Thoughts: _____

_____

_____

☐ **Today's Text: Romans 15:1-6** *(key v. 5)*

22 Today's Truth: "Like-minded" is the blessed characteristic of believers who are being conformed into Christ's image. By grace, God grants this harmony to those who walk with their gaze fixed on the Prince of Peace.

Today's Thoughts: _____

_____

_____

☐ **Today's Text: Romans 15:7-12** *(key v.7)*

23 Today's Truth. If we all diligently applied to our family life and marriage those principles that govern our walk as Christians, divorce rates would plummet, and the home would be the happiest place on earth. "Receive one another" in this text is an *aggressive* act of acceptance.

Today's Thoughts: _____

_____

_____

☐ **Today's Text: Romans 15:13-19** *(key v. 13)*

24 Today's Truth: As Christians, we serve "*the* God of hope." He is able to enter any situation of apparent "hopelesness" and work miracles. Redeeming His people from despair is second nature to the Almighty.

Today's Thoughts: _____

_____

_____

☐ **Today's Text: Romans 15:20-26** *(key v. 20)*

25 Today's Truth: Paul sought to bring the Gospel to spiritually dry places; locations where people were ignorant of the Good News. For most of us, this doesn't require travelling to a foreign mission field. Think of one person at work or in your neighborhood who needs to hear about Jesus and target a lunchtime with them to share your faith.

Today's Thoughts: _____

_____

_____

☐ **Today's Text: Romans 15:27-33** *(key v. 30)*

26 Today's Truth: When we see a spiritual giant such as the Apostle Paul *begging* for prayer, it is a reminder to us how dependent we all are on each other's spiritual support.

Today's Thoughts: _____

_____

_____

☐ **Today's Text: Romans 16:1-6** *(key v. 1)*

27 Today's Truth: Phoebe's name means "pure or radiant as the moon." This woman was obviously a brilliant reflection of the image and light of Jesus Christ. According to many scholars, it was this woman who carried this epistle of Paul to the congregation in Rome.

Today's Thoughts: _____

_____

_____

Today's Text: Romans 16:7-13 *(key v. 7)*

28 **Today's Truth:** The long list of Paul's greetings illustrates that he was not a leader who functioned in "authority at a distance," but he was one who cultivated intimate relationships with those he led.

Today's Thoughts: _____

_____

_____

☐ **Today's Text: Romans 16:14-20** *(key v.20)*

29 **Today's Truth:** The glorious promise of God to "crush Satan under our feet shortly" is predicated on our obedience and being innocent ("simple") with regard to evil (vs. 19). Note the teamwork involved: God will do the crushing but He will use our feet!

Today's Thoughts: _____

_____

_____

☐ **Today's Text: Romans 16:21-24** *(key v. 24)*

30 **Today's Truth:** There is power in pronouncing a blessing upon another person. Even the simplest words such as "the grace of our Lord Jesus Christ be with you" minister with a surprising degree of impact. This calls to mind that "Death and life are in the power of the tongue" (Prov. 18:21)

Today's Thoughts: _____

_____

_____

91

☐ **Today's Text: Romans 16:25-27** *(key v. 26)*

31 **Today's Truth:** It seems that Paul was almost able to close his letter in verse 24, but with one more final burst of praise and glorification of God, he pronounces his benediction. And with it, he reminds the reader that the glorious Gospel, amplified so magnificently in this Book of Romans, is commanded by God to be made known to every nation on earth in order that as many as are willing might know the Savior.

Today's Thoughts: ——————————

——————————————————————

——————————————————————

Additional Resources for Biblical Manhood. . .

BOOKS

A MAN'S STARTING PLACE

This first book in the "Power-To-Become" Book-Pak series is a study of how men become mature in Christ through relationships with God, their spouse, and with other men.*

Book only: AMSP $3.95
Book & Tape: BP01 $7.95

A MAN'S CONFIDENCE

This second book in the "Power-To-Become" Book-Pak series is a study of how men become confident in life through mastering guilt.*

Book only: AMC $3.95
Book & Tape: BP02 $7.95

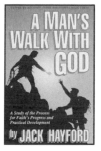

A MAN'S WALK WITH GOD

This third book in the "Power-To-Become" Book-Pak series is an exploration of the process for faith's progress and practical development.*

Book only: AMWG $3.95
Book & Tape: BP03 $7.95

* For subscription orders or quantity discounts for the "Power-To-Become" Books or Book-Pak series for use in personal or group studies, call (818) 779-8180 or (800) 776-8180.

GLORY ON YOUR HOUSE

Expanding upon the principles first set forth in his book, The Church On The Way, Jack Hayford explains how we can reflect God's glory. In this nearly 300-page book, he reminds us that we cannot expect blessings when we neglect our Father or grow indifferent to sin; only through a conscious effort to spend time with Him and carry out His will can we bring God's glory home. *(Chosen Books, hardback)*

Regularly $14.95   **GYH $12.95**

NEWBORN

This book outlines the basic elements in a growing life with Jesus and discusses the believer's relationship to God, how the Bible can help in one's spiritual journey, types of baptism, and the need for spending time with other believers.   **NBN $3.95**

SPIRIT-FILLED: The Overflowing Power of the Holy Spirit

Practical instruction on the Person and Power of the Spirit, teaching the enablement and resources of spiritual gifts and graces. Encourages the reader to open to the fullness of the Spirit of Christ, and shows how to maintain wisdom and balance in daily Spirit-filled living.   **SFL $3.95**

PRAYERPATH

Pastor Hayford takes the reader step by step along the pathway of prayer, examining the things Jesus taught about how to live and grow in vital faith, as well as how to pray for spiritual breakthrough at a global dimension. **PRP $3.95**

TAKING HOLD OF TOMORROW

The practical principles of "Possessing the Promised Land," found in the story of Joshua, encourage the reader to move forward and actively take hold of God's promises in life. This Angel Award winning book teaches the believer about spiritual warfare, submission, personal holiness, and obedience. *(Regularly $12.95)* **THT $9.95**

This same subject is presented in an 8-tape audio album and in a series of 4 videotapes.

Audio SC130 $34   Video PYTVS $65

REBUILDING THE REAL YOU

Just as Nehemiah went to Jerusalem with all the provisions he would need to rebuild the walls of the city, so the Holy Spirit comes with all that is needed to restore a broken personality. *(Regularly $8.95)* **RRY02 $7.95**

The same subject is presented in 11 audio tapes or 6 videotapes. **Audio SC046 $49.00**
Video RTWVS $99.00

AUDIO CASSETTE MINI-ALBUMS (2 tapes)

Honest to God	SC122	$8
Redeeming Relationships for Men & Women	SC177	$8
Why Sex Sins Are Worse Than Others	SC179	$8
How God Uses Men	SC223	$8
A Father's Approval	SC225	$8
Resisting the Devil	SC231	$8
How to Recession-Proof Your Home	SC369	$8
Safe Sex!	SC448	$8
The Leader Jesus Trusts	SC461	$8

AUDIO CASSETTE ALBUMS (# of tapes)

Cleansed for the Master's Use (3)	SC377	$13
Becoming God's Man (4)	SC457	$17
Fixing Family Fractures (4)	SC217	$17
The Power of Blessing (4)	SC395	$17
Men's Seminars 1990-91 (10)	MSEM	$42
Premarital Series (12)	PM02	$50
A Family Encyclopedia (24)	SC233	$99

VHS VIDEO ALBUMS

Why Sex Sins Are Worse Than Others	WSSV	$19
Divorce and the People of God	DIVV	$19
Earthly Search for a Heavenly Father	ESFV	$19

Add 15% for shipping and handling.
California residents add 8.25% sales tax.

Request your free Resource Catalog.

**Call Living Way Ministries Resources
at (818) 779-8180 or (800) 776-8180.**